HOW TO USE THIS BOOK

Many children dream of living on a farm
surrounded by their favourite animals.
This book encourages children to learn the
names of farm animals and their young, and
points to the important role each animal plays on
the farm.
Work through the book helping your child
identify the names of the animals and exploring
why they are important to the farmer.

Linda Coates, Cert Ed, MA

Animals on the Farm

written by Nina Filipek
illustrated by Louise Barrell

Filmset in Nelson Teaching Alphabet
by kind permission of
Thomas Nelson and Sons Ltd

Published in Great Britain by World International Publishing Limited,
An Egmont Company, Egmont House, P.O. Box I I I,
Great Ducie Street, Manchester M60 3BL.
Printed in Italy. SBN 7235 8868 6

The farmer keeps cows for their milk.
Cows are milked twice a day, once in the morning and once in the evening.
The milk is then sent to the dairy.

Cows eat a lot of grass.
Baby cows are called calves.

The farmer keeps sheep for their wool.
Sheep have a thick coat which is called a fleece.
In summer, the sheep are brought down from the hillside to be sheared.
Their coats are then sold and made into wool.

Baby sheep are called lambs.

Sheepdogs help the farmer move his sheep.
They are trained to understand the farmer's commands.

Long ago, the farmer would have kept horses to pull heavy ploughs and carts.
Nowadays, the farmer uses machinery to do this and doesn't need horses anymore.
Today, farmers keep horses as pets.

This is a foal, a baby horse.

The farmer sometimes keeps goats for their milk.

Goats' milk is used to make cheese and yoghurt.

Goats will eat almost anything they can find so the farmer usually keeps them tied up.

Do you know what a baby goat is called?

A baby goat is called a kid.

The farmer keeps chickens for their eggs.
Chickens feed on seeds and grains.
The mother is called a hen, the father is called a cockerel and the babies are called chicks.
How many fluffy yellow chicks can you see?

The farmer sometimes keeps turkeys.

Turkeys are big birds.
Like chickens, they have wings but
they cannot fly.

The farmer keeps ducks, too.
They like to swim and dive in the farmer's pond.
Notice their webbed feet.
Ducks eat fish, insects, worms and grasses.

Baby ducks are called ducklings.
They quickly learn to feed
themselves but it is a long time
before they can fly.

Here are some geese.
They live with the ducks on the farmer's pond.
Their babies are called goslings.
Like ducks, they can swim and fly.

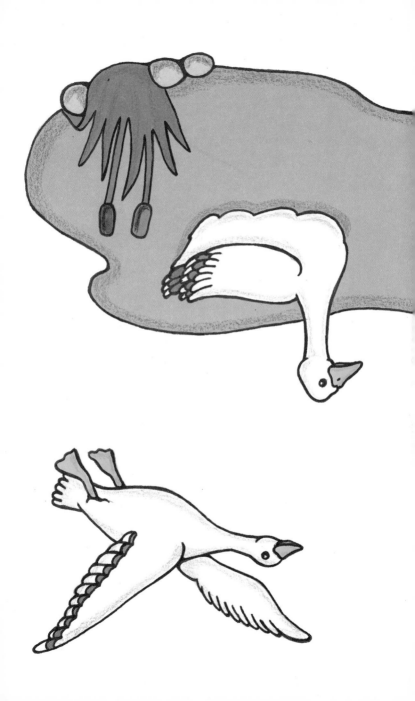

This is a farm cat.
She chases the mice from the barn.

Here are her babies.
They are called kittens.

Can you name all the animals the farmer keeps?

Name all the baby animals.

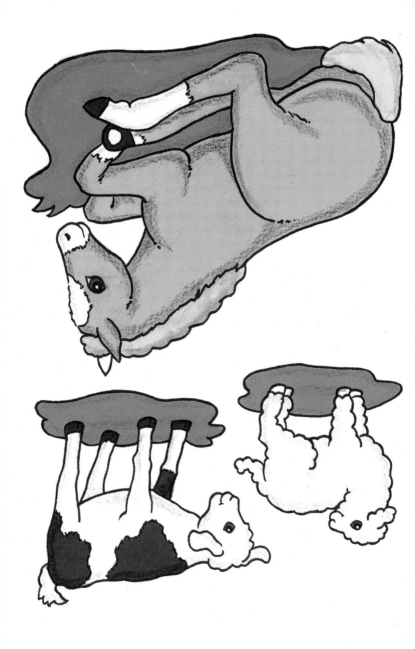